EMMANUEL JOSEPH

Faithful Foundations, Raising Godly Children with Entrepreneurial Spirits

Copyright © 2025 by Emmanuel Joseph

All rights reserved. No part of this publication may be reproduced, stored or transmitted in any form or by any means, electronic, mechanical, photocopying, recording, scanning, or otherwise without written permission from the publisher. It is illegal to copy this book, post it to a website, or distribute it by any other means without permission.

First edition

*This book was professionally typeset on Reedsy.
Find out more at reedsy.com*

Contents

1	Chapter 1: The Call to Parenthood	1
2	Chapter 2: Building a Strong Spiritual Foundation	3
3	Chapter 3: Cultivating a Growth Mindset	5
4	Chapter 4: Encouraging Financial Literacy	7
5	Chapter 5: Fostering Creativity and Innovation	9
6	Chapter 6: Teaching the Value of Hard Work and Perseverance	11
7	Chapter 7: Encouraging Entrepreneurial Thinking	13
8	Chapter 8: Teaching Effective Communication Skills	15
9	Chapter 9: Instilling a Sense of Responsibility and...	17
10	Chapter 10: Encouraging Teamwork and Collaboration	19
11	Chapter 11: Nurturing Emotional Intelligence	21
12	Chapter 12: Fostering a Sense of Gratitude and Humility	23
13	Chapter 13: Encouraging a Spirit of Service	25
14	Chapter 14: Developing Leadership Skills	27
15	Chapter 15: Balancing Faith and Ambition	29

1

Chapter 1: The Call to Parenthood

Parenthood is a divine vocation, a sacred call that transforms the lives of those who embrace it. When we decide to bring children into this world, we are entrusted with nurturing souls who will shape the future. The journey of raising godly children begins with the realization of this immense responsibility. One inspiring story is that of a young couple who, despite facing many obstacles, chose to adopt a child and raise her with love and faith. Their unwavering dedication and trust in God's plan resulted in a harmonious household that cultivated strong values and entrepreneurial aspirations.

As parents, our ultimate goal should be to cultivate an environment where faith flourishes and entrepreneurial spirits soar. We can draw inspiration from biblical figures such as Abraham and Sarah, who exemplified unwavering faith in God's promises. Their perseverance in the face of adversity serves as a testament to the power of divine trust. By following their example, we can guide our children towards a life rooted in faith and innovation.

The foundation of successful parenting lies in creating a strong bond with our children. This bond is forged through open communication, mutual respect, and unconditional love. We must strive to understand their unique personalities, interests, and talents, while also imparting essential life skills and values. Sharing personal anecdotes from our own faith journeys and entrepreneurial endeavors can serve as valuable lessons for our children.

In a rapidly changing world, it's crucial to equip our children with the tools they need to navigate life's challenges. This includes fostering a strong sense of faith and a resilient entrepreneurial spirit. By teaching them to trust in God and embrace their creativity, we empower them to become compassionate, resourceful, and innovative individuals. Let us embark on this journey with hearts full of faith and minds open to endless possibilities.

2

Chapter 2: Building a Strong Spiritual Foundation

The cornerstone of raising godly children is establishing a strong spiritual foundation. This begins with regular prayer and worship, as well as teaching our children the importance of a personal relationship with God. One memorable story is that of a single mother who, despite her busy schedule, made it a priority to pray with her children every night. Her consistent efforts instilled a deep sense of faith and devotion in her children, who grew up to become active members of their church community.

A crucial aspect of building a strong spiritual foundation is introducing our children to the teachings of the Bible. By sharing stories of faith, perseverance, and redemption, we can help them understand the importance of living according to God's will. Encouraging them to participate in church activities and Sunday school can further strengthen their spiritual growth and sense of belonging.

In addition to biblical teachings, it's essential to cultivate an atmosphere of gratitude and humility in our homes. By modeling these virtues, we can help our children develop a profound appreciation for God's blessings and a humble heart. One practical way to achieve this is by involving them in acts of service, such as volunteering at a local food bank or participating in community outreach programs. These experiences can teach them the value of selflessness and compassion.

As parents, we must also be mindful of our own spiritual growth. Our children look to us as role models, and our actions speak louder than words. By prioritizing our relationship with God and seeking His guidance in all aspects of our lives, we can set a powerful example for our children to follow. Let us commit to nurturing their spiritual growth with unwavering dedication and faith.

3

Chapter 3: Cultivating a Growth Mindset

A growth mindset is the belief that one's abilities and intelligence can be developed through dedication, hard work, and perseverance. This mindset is essential for fostering entrepreneurial spirits in our children. One inspiring example is that of a young boy who, despite struggling academically, discovered his passion for coding. With the support of his parents and a relentless determination, he went on to create a successful tech startup, proving that a growth mindset can lead to extraordinary achievements.

To cultivate a growth mindset in our children, we must encourage them to embrace challenges and view failures as opportunities for growth. This involves praising their efforts rather than their innate abilities and teaching them the value of persistence and resilience. By celebrating their successes and learning from their setbacks, we can help them develop a strong sense of self-belief and determination.

In addition to fostering a growth mindset, it's important to provide our children with opportunities to explore their interests and passions. This can be achieved by exposing them to a variety of activities, such as sports, arts, and sciences, and encouraging them to pursue their curiosities. One memorable story is that of a young girl who, after attending a robotics workshop, discovered her love for engineering. With the unwavering support of her parents, she pursued her passion and eventually became a leading innovator in her field.

As parents, we must also model a growth mindset in our own lives. By demonstrating a willingness to learn, adapt, and grow, we can inspire our children to do the same. This can be achieved by setting personal goals, seeking new experiences, and embracing the unknown with courage and optimism. Let us commit to fostering a growth mindset in our children, empowering them to reach their full potential.

4

Chapter 4: Encouraging Financial Literacy

Financial literacy is a crucial skill for fostering entrepreneurial spirits in our children. By teaching them the basics of money management, saving, and investing, we can empower them to make informed financial decisions and achieve financial independence. One inspiring story is that of a teenager who, with the guidance of his parents, started a small business selling handmade crafts. Through this experience, he learned valuable lessons about budgeting, profit margins, and customer service, ultimately developing a strong entrepreneurial mindset.

To encourage financial literacy in our children, we must start with the basics. This includes teaching them the importance of saving and the concept of delayed gratification. One practical way to achieve this is by giving them a weekly allowance and encouraging them to set aside a portion of it for savings. Over time, they will learn the value of saving for future goals and the satisfaction that comes from achieving them.

In addition to saving, it's essential to teach our children about budgeting and responsible spending. This can be achieved by involving them in family financial discussions and showing them how to create a budget. By demonstrating the importance of tracking expenses and making informed financial decisions, we can help them develop sound money management skills.

Investing is another crucial aspect of financial literacy. By introducing our children to the concept of investing and the power of compound interest, we can help them understand the benefits of growing their wealth over time. One memorable story is that of a young girl who, with the guidance of her parents, started investing a portion of her allowance in a savings account. Over the years, she watched her savings grow, ultimately inspiring her to explore other investment opportunities.

As parents, we must also model responsible financial behavior in our own lives. By demonstrating the importance of saving, budgeting, and investing, we can set a powerful example for our children to follow. Let us commit to teaching our children the principles of financial literacy, empowering them to achieve financial independence and success.

Chapter 5: Fostering Creativity and Innovation

Creativity and innovation are essential qualities for nurturing entrepreneurial spirits in our children. By encouraging them to think outside the box and explore new ideas, we can help them develop a strong sense of creativity and problem-solving skills. One inspiring story is that of a young boy who, with the support of his parents, turned his love for drawing into a successful online business. Through this experience, he learned valuable lessons about creativity, marketing, and customer engagement.

To foster creativity and innovation in our children, we must provide them with opportunities to explore their interests and passions. This can be achieved by exposing them to a variety of activities, such as arts, sciences, and technology, and encouraging them to pursue their curiosities. One memorable story is that of a young girl who, after attending a science fair, discovered her love for chemistry. With the unwavering support of her parents, she pursued her passion and eventually became a leading innovator in her field.

In addition to providing opportunities for exploration, it's important to create an environment that encourages creative thinking and problem-solving. This involves praising their efforts, celebrating their successes, and learning from their setbacks. By fostering a growth mindset and encouraging them to view challenges as opportunities for growth, we can help them develop a strong sense of self-belief and determination.

As parents, we must also model creativity and innovation in our own lives. By demonstrating a willingness to learn, adapt, and grow, we can inspire our children to do the same. This can be achieved by setting personal goals, seeking new experiences, and embracing the unknown with courage and optimism. Let us commit to fostering creativity and innovation in our children, empowering them to become resourceful, inventive, and successful individuals.

6

Chapter 6: Teaching the Value of Hard Work and Perseverance

Hard work and perseverance are essential qualities for nurturing entrepreneurial spirits in our children. By teaching them the importance of dedication and persistence, we can help them develop a strong work ethic and a resilient mindset. One inspiring story is that of a young boy who, with the guidance of his parents, turned his passion for baking into a successful home-based business. Through this experience, he learned valuable lessons about hard work, time management, and customer satisfaction.

To teach the value of hard work and perseverance, we must start with the basics. This includes setting clear expectations and providing consistent guidance and support. One practical way to achieve this is by assigning age-appropriate chores and responsibilities, which can help our children develop a sense of accountability and discipline.

In addition to chores, it's important to provide opportunities for our children to engage in activities that require dedication and perseverance. This can include sports, music, or academic pursuits. One memorable story is that of a young girl who, after struggling with her piano lessons, decided to practice diligently and eventually mastered the instrument. Her journey of perseverance and hard work serves as a powerful example of what can be achieved through dedication and commitment.

As parents, we must also model hard work and perseverance in our own lives. By demonstrating a strong work ethic and a willingness to develop new skills, we can set a powerful example for our children. By pursuing our own goals with dedication and perseverance, we can inspire them to do the same. Let us commit to teaching our children the value of hard work and perseverance, empowering them to achieve their dreams.

7

Chapter 7: Encouraging Entrepreneurial Thinking

Entrepreneurial thinking involves recognizing opportunities, taking calculated risks, and developing innovative solutions. By encouraging our children to think like entrepreneurs, we can help them develop a proactive and resourceful mindset. One inspiring story is that of a young boy who, with the support of his parents, started a neighborhood lawn care service. Through this experience, he learned valuable lessons about business planning, customer relations, and financial management.

To encourage entrepreneurial thinking, we must provide our children with opportunities to explore their interests and passions. This can be achieved by exposing them to a variety of activities, such as business clubs, entrepreneurship programs, and hands-on projects. One memorable story is that of a young girl who, after attending a business camp, discovered her love for entrepreneurship. With the unwavering support of her parents, she pursued her passion and eventually launched a successful online store.

In addition to providing opportunities for exploration, it's important to create an environment that encourages creative thinking and problem-solving. This involves praising their efforts, celebrating their successes, and learning from their setbacks. By fostering a growth mindset and encouraging them to view challenges as opportunities for growth, we can help them develop a strong sense of self-belief and determination.

As parents, we must also model entrepreneurial thinking in our own lives. By demonstrating a willingness to take risks, embrace new ideas, and adapt to changing circumstances, we can inspire our children to do the same. This can be achieved by setting personal goals, seeking new experiences, and embracing the unknown with courage and optimism. Let us commit to encouraging entrepreneurial thinking in our children, empowering them to become innovative, resourceful, and successful individuals.

8

Chapter 8: Teaching Effective Communication Skills

Effective communication is a vital skill for nurturing entrepreneurial spirits in our children. By teaching them the importance of clear and confident communication, we can help them build strong relationships and successfully convey their ideas. One inspiring story is that of a young girl who, with the guidance of her parents, joined a public speaking club. Through this experience, she developed her communication skills and gained the confidence to present her business ideas to potential investors.

To teach effective communication skills, we must start with the basics. This includes encouraging our children to express their thoughts and feelings openly and respectfully. One practical way to achieve this is by engaging in regular family discussions and actively listening to their opinions. By creating an open and supportive environment, we can help them develop strong communication skills.

In addition to family discussions, it's important to provide opportunities for our children to practice their communication skills in various settings. This can include public speaking, debates, and group projects. One memorable story is that of a young boy who, after participating in a school debate, discovered his passion for persuasive communication. With the unwavering support of his parents, he pursued his interest and eventually became a skilled orator and successful entrepreneur.

As parents, we must also model effective communication in our own lives. By demonstrating active listening, empathy, and clarity in our interactions, we can set a powerful example for our children to follow. Let us commit to teaching our children the principles of effective communication, empowering them to build strong relationships and convey their ideas with confidence.

9

Chapter 9: Instilling a Sense of Responsibility and Accountability

A sense of responsibility and accountability is essential for nurturing entrepreneurial spirits in our children. By teaching them the importance of taking ownership of their actions and decisions, we can help them develop a strong sense of integrity and reliability. One inspiring story is that of a young boy who, with the guidance of his parents, took on the responsibility of managing the family's garden. Through this experience, he learned valuable lessons about responsibility, time management, and accountability.

To instill a sense of responsibility and accountability, we must start with the basics. This includes assigning age-appropriate chores and responsibilities and providing consistent guidance and support. One practical way to achieve this is by involving our children in household tasks, such as cleaning, cooking, and caring for pets. By giving them the opportunity to contribute to the family's well-being, we can help them develop a sense of responsibility and accountability.

In addition to household tasks, it's important to provide opportunities for our children to take on responsibilities in various settings. This can include school projects, extracurricular activities, and volunteer work. One memorable story is that of a young girl who, after volunteering at a local animal shelter, discovered her passion for animal welfare. With the unwavering support of her parents, she pursued her interest and eventually became a dedicated advocate for animal rights.

As parents, we must also model responsibility and accountability in our own lives. By demonstrating a strong work ethic, reliability, and integrity, we can set a powerful example for our children to follow. Let us commit to instilling a sense of responsibility and accountability in our children, empowering them to become trustworthy, dependable, and successful individuals.

10

Chapter 10: Encouraging Teamwork and Collaboration

Teamwork and collaboration are essential skills for nurturing entrepreneurial spirits in our children. By teaching them the importance of working together and valuing diverse perspectives, we can help them develop strong interpersonal skills and a collaborative mindset. One inspiring story is that of a young boy who, with the guidance of his parents, joined a robotics team. Through this experience, he learned valuable lessons about teamwork, problem-solving, and innovation.

To encourage teamwork and collaboration, we must provide our children with opportunities to work with others. This can include group projects, team sports, and collaborative activities. One practical way to achieve this is by involving our children in family projects, such as planning a vacation or organizing a community event. By working together towards a common goal, we can help them develop a strong sense of teamwork and collaboration.

In addition to family projects, it's important to provide opportunities for our children to engage in teamwork and collaboration in various settings. This can include school clubs, extracurricular activities, and community organizations. One memorable story is that of a young girl who, after joining a community theater group, discovered her love for performing arts. With the unwavering support of her parents, she pursued her passion and eventually became a talented actress and successful entrepreneur.

As parents, we must also model teamwork and collaboration in our own lives. By demonstrating a willingness to work with others, value diverse perspectives, and contribute to shared goals, we can set a powerful example for our children to follow. Let us commit to encouraging teamwork and collaboration in our children, empowering them to become cooperative, resourceful, and successful individuals.

11

Chapter 11: Nurturing Emotional Intelligence

Emotional intelligence is the ability to recognize, understand, and manage our own emotions and the emotions of others. By nurturing emotional intelligence in our children, we can help them develop strong interpersonal skills and a resilient mindset. One inspiring story is that of a young boy who, with the guidance of his parents, learned to manage his anxiety through mindfulness and meditation. Through this experience, he developed a greater sense of self-awareness and emotional regulation.

To nurture emotional intelligence, we must start with the basics. This includes teaching our children to recognize and name their emotions and providing strategies for managing them. One practical way to achieve this is by engaging in regular family discussions about emotions and encouraging our children to express their feelings openly and respectfully.

In addition to family discussions, it's important to provide opportunities for our children to practice emotional intelligence in various settings. This can include social interactions, group activities, and conflict resolution. One memorable story is that of a young girl who, after participating in a school peer mediation program, discovered her passion for helping others resolve conflicts. With the unwavering support of her parents, she pursued her interest and eventually became a skilled mediator and successful entrepreneur.

As parents, we must also model emotional intelligence in our own lives. By demonstrating empathy, self-awareness, and effective communication, we can set a powerful example for our children to follow. Let us commit to nurturing emotional intelligence in our children, empowering them to build strong relationships, manage their emotions, and achieve success.

12

Chapter 12: Fostering a Sense of Gratitude and Humility

Gratitude and humility are essential qualities for nurturing godly children with entrepreneurial spirits. By teaching our children the importance of being grateful and humble, we can help them develop a profound appreciation for God's blessings and a grounded perspective on success. One inspiring story is that of a young girl who, with the guidance of her parents, started a gratitude journal. Through this practice, she learned to recognize and appreciate the small blessings in her life, ultimately developing a grateful and humble heart.

To foster a sense of gratitude and humility, we must start with the basics. This includes modeling these virtues in our own lives and encouraging our children to practice gratitude regularly. One practical way to achieve this is by incorporating gratitude into our daily routines, such as sharing what we are thankful for during family meals or bedtime prayers.

In addition to practicing gratitude, it's important to teach our children the value of humility. This involves recognizing our own limitations, appreciating the contributions of others, and maintaining a grounded perspective on success. One memorable story is that of a young boy who, after achieving success in a school competition, chose to share the credit with his teammates and mentors. His humble attitude and acknowledgment of others' support served as a powerful example of humility.

As parents, we must also model gratitude and humility in our own lives. By demonstrating a grateful and humble attitude, we can set a powerful example for our children to follow. Let us commit to fostering a sense of gratitude and humility in our children, empowering them to develop a profound appreciation for God's blessings and a grounded perspective on success.

13

Chapter 13: Encouraging a Spirit of Service

A spirit of service is essential for nurturing godly children with entrepreneurial spirits. By teaching our children the importance of serving others, we can help them develop a compassionate and selfless mindset. One inspiring story is that of a young boy who, with the guidance of his parents, started a community garden project. Through this experience, he learned the value of service, teamwork, and making a positive impact on his community.

To encourage a spirit of service, we must provide our children with opportunities to serve others. This can include volunteer work, community service projects, and acts of kindness. One practical way to achieve this is by involving our children in family service projects, such as organizing a neighborhood cleanup or volunteering at a local shelter. By working together to serve others, we can help them develop a compassionate and selfless mindset.

In addition to family service projects, it's important to provide opportunities for our children to engage in service in various settings. This can include school clubs, extracurricular activities, and community organizations. One memorable story is that of a young girl who, after participating in a school charity drive, discovered her passion for helping others. With the unwavering support of her parents, she pursued her interest and eventually became a dedicated philanthropist and successful entrepreneur.

As parents, we must also model a spirit of service in our own lives. By demonstrating a willingness to serve others and make a positive impact on our communities, we can set a powerful example for our children to follow. Let us commit to encouraging a spirit of service in our children, empowering them to become compassionate, selfless, and successful individuals.

14

Chapter 14: Developing Leadership Skills

Leadership skills are essential for nurturing entrepreneurial spirits in our children. By teaching them the importance of leading with integrity, empathy, and vision, we can help them develop strong leadership qualities. One inspiring story is that of a young boy who, with the guidance of his parents, took on a leadership role in his school's student council. Through this experience, he learned valuable lessons about responsibility, teamwork, and effective communication.

To develop leadership skills in our children, we must provide opportunities for them to take on leadership roles. This can include school projects, extracurricular activities, and community organizations. One practical way to achieve this is by encouraging our children to lead family activities, such as planning a vacation or organizing a family game night. By giving them the opportunity to take charge and make decisions, we can help them develop strong leadership skills.

In addition to providing leadership opportunities, it's important to teach our children the principles of effective leadership. This includes leading by example, communicating clearly, and valuing the contributions of others. One memorable story is that of a young girl who, after attending a leadership camp, discovered her passion for leading and inspiring others. With the unwavering support of her parents, she pursued her interest and eventually became a respected leader and successful entrepreneur.

As parents, we must also model effective leadership in our own lives. By demonstrating integrity, empathy, and vision in our actions, we can set a powerful example for our children to follow. Let us commit to developing leadership skills in our children, empowering them to become confident, compassionate, and successful leaders.

15

Chapter 15: Balancing Faith and Ambition

Balancing faith and ambition is essential for raising godly children with entrepreneurial spirits. By teaching our children the importance of aligning their goals with their faith, we can help them develop a balanced and fulfilling life. One inspiring story is that of a young girl who, with the guidance of her parents, pursued her dream of becoming a successful business owner while staying true to her faith. Through this experience, she learned valuable lessons about integrity, purpose, and trusting in God's plan.

To balance faith and ambition, we must start with the basics. This includes teaching our children to set goals that align with their values and faith. One practical way to achieve this is by involving them in regular discussions about their aspirations and how they can honor God through their endeavors. By encouraging them to seek God's guidance in their decision-making, we can help them develop a balanced and purpose-driven mindset.

In addition to goal-setting, it's important to teach our children the value of trusting in God's plan. This involves recognizing that success is not solely defined by material achievements, but by living a life that honors God and serves others. One memorable story is that of a young boy who, despite facing numerous setbacks in his entrepreneurial journey, remained steadfast in his faith and trusted in God's plan. His unwavering trust and perseverance eventually led to success beyond his wildest dreams.

As parents, we must also model the balance of faith and ambition in our own lives. By demonstrating a commitment to our faith while pursuing our goals, we can set a powerful example for our children to follow. Let us commit to balancing faith and ambition in our children, empowering them to achieve their dreams while staying true to their values and faith.

Faithful Foundations: Raising Godly Children with Entrepreneurial Spirits is a compelling guide for parents who aspire to nurture their children's faith and entrepreneurial mindset. This book provides a practical and heartfelt approach to parenting, combining timeless biblical principles with modern strategies for fostering creativity, financial literacy, leadership skills, and emotional intelligence.

Through inspiring stories and real-life examples, "Faithful Foundations" illustrates the transformative power of faith and hard work. Each chapter offers valuable insights and actionable advice on building a strong spiritual foundation, cultivating a growth mindset, and encouraging entrepreneurial thinking. From teaching effective communication skills to balancing faith and ambition, this book covers a wide range of topics essential for raising well-rounded, godly children.

By following the guidance in "Faithful Foundations," parents can create an environment that promotes faith, innovation, and a sense of responsibility. This book empowers families to embark on a journey of spiritual and entrepreneurial growth, ultimately preparing their children to thrive in all aspects of life.

www.ingramcontent.com/pod-product-compliance
Lightning Source LLC
LaVergne TN
LVHW020501080526
838202LV00057B/6099